Caught
Heart

Caught Heart

Poems

Noreen Norris

SUNSTONE PRESS

SANTA FE

July 11, 2009
For Janet,
In memory of our
family times together.
Love,
cousin Noreen

On the cover: *Moonrise Over Abiquiu*, a watercolor
by Marian A. Shirin from the author's collection.

Sunstone books may be purchased for educational, business, or sales promotional use.
For information please write: Special Markets Department, Sunstone Press,
P.O. Box 2321, Santa Fe, New Mexico 87504-2321.

Book and Cover design › Vicki Ahl
Body typeface › Goudy Old Style ◆ Display type › Goudy Handtooled BT
Printed on acid free paper

Library of Congress Cataloging-in-Publication Data

Norris, Noreen, 1937-
Caught heart : poems / by Noreen Norris.
p. cm.
ISBN 978-0-86534-655-0 (pbk. : alk. paper)
I. Title.
PS3614.O769C38 2009
811'.6--dc22
2009002029

WWW.SUNSTONEPRESS.COM
SUNSTONE PRESS / POST OFFICE BOX 2321 / SANTA FE, NM 87504-2321 /USA
(505) 988-4418 / ORDERS ONLY (800) 243-5644 / FAX (505) 988-1025

To Michael Scofield, my loving husband, for helping me
find my way to this book.

And Thanks To:

The editors of the following journals, where some of
the poems in this collection have previously appeared:
Diner: "Snow Country," "The Kiss,"; *Sin Fronteras/Writers
Without Borders*: Sixty Years Ago" (under the title "Fifty
Years Ago"); *The Comstock Review*: "Holding On."

Michael Scofield for copyediting, and to poets Dana
Levin and Carol Moldaw for lending their insight and
clarification to the reworking of many of these poems.

Oh friend! When the timbers fall,
don't buy more crooked nails;
buy a tiny mirror to take home.

Contents

Preface - - 11

Glide to White - - 13

I
Stand Up

The Kiss - - 17
Stand Up - - 18
1942 - - 19
1943 - - 20
behind a cloud drift - - 21
snowmelt - - 22
The Danube: 1944 - - 23
Picking Berries - - 24
American Beauty - - 25
Babylon— - - 28
Zinnias - - 29
summer afternoon - - 30
The Rowboat - - 31
sun high— - - 32
Under the noontime sun - - 33
Epidemic: 1949 - - 34
cold autumn lake: - - 35
The Well House - - 36
frozen lake . . . - - 38
having finished the ice fort - - 39
Snow Country - - 40

cutting through - - 41
A Bad Bet - - 42
Detroit: First Generation - - 43
ritual: - - 44
Sixty Years Ago - - 45
March ice: - - 46
The Pretty Toys - - 47
too steep - - 49

II
Walking On Ice

From the hand-bound book - - 53
Rain - - 54
July thunder - - 55
Holding On - - 56
We need - - 57
Fools - - 58
Safety - - 60
moving day - - 61
Flight - - 62
The Tryout - - 63
little girl - - 64
Taking You Home - - 65
dapple-gray ponies - - 66
The Litchfield Hatchery - - 67
tart McIntosh— - - 69
On the Road - - 70
On Wishing Myself a New Life - - 71
Dry leaves crumble - - 73
Lost - - 74
snowdrift, - - 75
The lake ice glares, - - 76
Walking on Ice - - 77

III
Foot Soldiers

sun kisses the wings - - 81
Maytime - - 82
our love came - - 83
Il Divino - - 84
in Donnini Forest - - 85
Starfish brighten - - 86
meadowlark— - - 87
missing signs - - 88
Mouse Tales - - 89
In Search of Kasey - - 90
Foot Soldiers - - 91
old cherry tree, - - 92
School Days - - 93
On winter nights, dense fog - - 95
again this year - - 96
The Jump - - 97
crows - - 98
Deepest Dark - - 99
Judgment Day - - 101
No One Sees - - 102

IV
How Gentleness Came

let bitter wind - - 105
At China Cove - - 106
plunging neckline— - - 108
A Visit from God - - 109
Blown in wide circles - - 111
raindrops on windows— - - 112
Status - - 113

real estate boom - - 114
The Embrace - - 115
evening stroll . . . - - 116
burning desert gusts - - 117
Endgame - - 118
deep autumn . . . - - 119
coyotes yelp - - 120
on and on the clouds . . . - - 121
A Black Heaven - - 122
from my sickbed - - 123
bomb's whistle— - - 124
wounded desert lark: - - 125
No End in Sight - - 126
Iraq . . . - - 127
Light - - 128
steady slant of rain - - 129
holy water: - - 130
how like - - 131
Contentment - - 132
how simple . . . - - 133
The Way Gentleness Came - - 134
startled— - - 136
after twenty years - - 137
First Blossoms - - 138
for just a moment - - 139

And with Fondness... - - 140

Preface

Since age four, when my mother taught me to memorize and recite children's poetry, the sounds and rhythms of all kinds of styles and voices have come to haunt me. In *Caught Heart* I use the language of lyrical and prose poems, as well as the immediate awareness of haiku, senryu, and hibiki to make sense of the mind—never in control, trying always to integrate dark with light.

My subject is daily life. I write about lakes and rivers and the sea, family and friends and enemies, the ways of the sun and moon, and especially about the seasons— nature's and my own. None of this is new to poetry. But, hopefully, the reader's imagination will see reflected here the vulnerable psyche. For each person must find her or his own truth, even as so many choose to stay in spiritual slumber.

As a Pisces, I hear, feel, and see existence as an inward experience, allowing the translation of actual reality into personal truth, however surreal. These poems echo the cosmic pain entrusted to each of us and the joy of overcoming bitterness that may come from that pain.

I: Recaptures beginnings in Michigan, where the beauty of ordinary things and people formed my understanding of the larger world. Ordinary people for me were workers and farmers rather than the elite. The quiet strength that many of the poems propose comes from the introverted Swedes and Norwegians of my father's family. Mother's French family loved to change words into pictures drawn with plenty of emotion.

In May of 1959 after graduation from Detroit's Wayne State University with a degree in speech and in sociology, I moved to California and learned to relax in the Bay Area's kinder weather. Here my two children demonstrated why our questions can never fully be answered.

II: Details the painful end of twenty-five years near and in Palo Alto, followed by a nine-month return to Michigan to aid my dying father.

III: Returns me to Palo Alto, where my second husband and I shared a comfortable life for a decade. But we became too adept at producing marketing documents for executives in Silicon Valley—and burned out. Family members as well as friends began to experience deep suffering. Our little city soon personified the "boom" of the 1990's.

IV: Reveals the rebirth we felt on moving to Santa Fe in 1995—we still cherish the vivid earth colors and power of the light. Here we also share the challenge to live in wisdom and compassion and gratitude for earth:

oh, ancient river!

—Noreen Norris
Santa Fe

Glide to White

pity finds her way
terror delights in
deceit steps quietly
desire feels her need
jealousy dresses with
anger remains untouched
sorrow poses as

through tears
icy air
into fear
for fire
greatest care
and fair
loving care

the unclouded moon
on who they are
which shadow
invites me now

spreads its light
which type
rules my night
to glide to white

I

Stand Up

The Kiss

When I walk
slowly into the lake
in the afternoon sun,
my liquid legs cool,
and I know why fish tremble
when we yank them
into the air—
only this silky coldness
thrills them, caresses them,
kisses their large lips.

As I swim
evenly into this bliss,
under the white sun,
my body sighs,
and suddenly I think of how Jochebed
set Moses
afloat on the Nile—
feel that black river lift
the babe, lull him,
kiss his basket.

I'm not kidding myself—
I don't want
to be a fish,
to hide in the kiss,
only to vanish in this clear water
until my caught heart rises.

Stand Up

"Stand up," the wind screams.
"Stand up and meet this day
like any other."

It's only a small death after all.

1942

We might find ourselves
again and live like men of
peace, could we think
which way to look.

Until then, let's build fires
to celebrate the fun we have
singing "Bell Bottom Trousers"
on the front-porch swing.

1943

Mary heard Jake open the front door. She was in the kitchen in the back of the house, snapping beans into a bucket in the metal sink, when she felt him come close and lean silently against the yellow doorjamb. She hummed a hymn, snapping the beans in time. Soon his own humming became loud enough for her to hear. She turned to smile at him—but he had gone.

The afternoon lagged. The porcelain tabletop needed wiping, and there were still some berries to pick. Then it would be time for supper. "You'd sure get a kick out of me tryin' ta eat this bumper crop of beans," she said to Jake's photo on the sideboard. Tomorrow morning she'd wash the window where his gold star hung.

behind a cloud drift

the moon has stopped—

clever move

snowmelt

slows their steps—

the last train

The Danube: 1944

There is silence
there is silence here

there is silence
where was sound

gunning down of sound
where tears were

there is silence
gunning down

silence

Picking Berries

Between the world wars, Dad and his brothers built their family a stone cottage with a wall behind to retain a sandy bank. By the summer of 1944, raspberry and blackberry bushes owned every acre beyond that wall all the way to the woods, and my cousin Jack was in Normandy. Grandma and I got ready before the sun was too hot. She said she needed my help if she was to have enough berries for pies and jam.

"Put this apron on ya," she said, wrapping the ties twice around my middle. Then, she pulled half sleeves cut from grandpa's old sweater up my lower arms as a shield. "Now," she exclaimed, hooking a tin bucket on my fingers, "we'll git us some berries. Let yer cousin pick off Hitler's hoodlums over there in France. Best put on these too," she said, handing me a pair of cotton gloves. "Them thorns 'r devils."

American Beauty

1

Long-stemmed roses
bared their bleeding gums,
snapped the notes that flew
over a crystal vase
atop the baby grand.
A fresh-ironed pinafore
clung to my thighs,
damp Shirley Temple curls
brushed my neck,
and I knew I was special,
invited into this room
crowded with grownups
to see a fragile
blond nine-year-old
play perfect Mozart
over the whir of the fan
placed on the stool next to him.

I could feel my cheeks flush
in the muggy room as the notes
came pouring out of those fingers.
The boy looked like a child,
but I knew he could not be one—
an angel then.

—continued

I caught a whiff
of the blood-red roses
the instant he lifted his hand,
nicked by the fan blade,
trailing crimson drops
along the keys.

The stained blade swirled;
the bright angel played on—
at last he turned,
stunned as any child,
his frightened eyes
asking our permission to stop.

2

And while I listened to him
play Mozart in Detroit,
on the outskirts of Bonn
a mad siren screamed
every night—
two minutes to run terrified,
my dear friend Gisela,
in your wrinkled dress
to the basement
of your apartment house,
the black cellar
crowded with neighbors,
while bombs kept you
from your bed.
Terror stuck in your throat

like some secret
too thick to hide.

Your mother prayed,
    "Angel of Mercy, tell us
                when it's enough."
You choked on the foul air,
on fear the sign of the cross
could not comfort,
felt your cheeks flame
as the fire came pouring down.
Hitler called himself German,
but you knew he could not be—
the devil, you decided.

Our bombs consumed the heart of Bonn
as you stood in the farthest corner,
still as death,
hands wet with perspiration—
begging us to stop.

Babylon—

hanging gardens

of despots' dreams

Zinnias

Aunt Cora said she saw the face of God every time she planted zinnia seeds, and that cutting the blossoms in August was like bringing His smile into the house. She put them in every room. Zinnias in her best ruby-red vase in the front hall repeated the red, orange, pink, and gold shining through the stained glass over the door.

The front parlor, where Cora's wood coffin stood for three days in August of 1944, burst with every zinnia grown in the town's gardens. "They're not really funeral flowers," whispered the young undertaker. "But son," Cora's niece sighed, "there's no other flower would do."

summer afternoon

distant childhood . . .

white goose by flashing lake

The Rowboat

I sat quite still, hands folded in my lap,
as I had sat each summer,
waiting for my time to have the key
off its hook, hung above my reach—
row the heavy boat alone.

Grandfather said that wooden oars required
a boy's arms to pull against. Yet, sitting silently
on the center seat for each day's drill,
he showed me how to row, his veined hand
on one, both of mine on the other oar—

until I knew enough and my arms grew strong.
He passed me the key a hot July day.
With quickening heart I walked the tar-soft road
past the dance hall near the shore, alone.

sun high—

fragrant water lilies open,

part for my fish-filled boat

Under the noontime sun
I laugh at fluttering butterflies
Beetles kissing my feet.

Going up to the sky in a Ferris wheel
We cannot bear to swing back to earth.

Epidemic: 1949

The heat of summer stirs us.
Tonight fireworks will salute the sky.
You slam the screen door and race upstairs
for your bathing suit, hoping today
you'll get to swim with friends.
We cannot guess what's to come,

that Father's dog-days, no-swim rule
will not protect you, that spasms will strike
by November. This day you are strong,
hepped up to celebrate the Fourth. No sign of
infantile paralysis—six months of Sister Kenny
hot packs. "Please, please, Dad," you beg.

Father says no to the creek. But you do not
hang your swimsuit back on its hook.
You put it on, sashay into our one bathroom,
fill the tub to the brim with cold water,
slide slowly down almost to your chin, peeved
even when the two-piece silk glows bright blue.

cold autumn lake:

atop its waters a lone duck

flies through blank sky

The Well House

No one knew why the young man
had hung himself.
No one would talk about it.

I went there with my sister,
through a dry field,
breaking the brown stiffness
of grass and weeds.
Darkened by heavy clouds,
the abandoned concrete well house
bordered the creek.
I squeezed my sister's hand
through her wool mitten,
and stared at the rotted roof,
tall, rust-streaked walls.

My sister pulled my arm,
pointed at the sky. The sun
had torn a cloud.
It threw enough light to turn
the raw walls hollow.

We stepped over the doorjamb
into the narrow room
and stared at the hole,
its rim become a halo.

How had he done it?
How flung the noose straight up
over this terrible pit?
My sister moved behind me,
hands grabbing my coat,
her face pressed to my back.

frozen lake . . .

a lone willow

weeps

having finished the ice fort

    inside

        our breath freezes to the walls

Snow Country

People in snow country use ice as money. It jingles in
their pockets and slips nicely into deerskin envelopes
to pay bills—overdue in the month of summer. Jacob
pulls his red sled to a stop. It is stacked high with
orange crates—ice glints through the slats. I want you
to share in my bounty, Jacob says. Then he thumps me
on the shoulder and turns me toward the First National
Ice Bank—just as I notice his initials etched into the end
of every slab.

cutting through

winter's icy silence—

the skater's blades

A Bad Bet

Four Scots and one Swede staring
at the icy river, wearing
hobnailed boots and hand-knit scarves,
four coal miners and a dirt farmer

who've forsaken their soil
to bury themselves at Ford's River Rouge
Assembly plant. A bad bet in this Detroit
on the edge of hating itself even before

the riots of '43, clamoring for Poles and
Italians, coming in by the boatload, to
stamp fenders on grinding swing shifts
to mortgage a gray, blue-collar life.

By '57, southern blacks working the line.
Laid off for good in December,
four Scots and a Swede staring out
at the ice on their driveways,

wearing their galoshes to east-side bars,
betting their savings on the Red Wings,
holing up in their half-finished basements
with their smokes and cases of Stroh's.

Detroit: First Generation

We collected pennies,
put them in piles—
when Johnny came marching home,
we slipped them into loafers
and danced all over town.

We're new, papà.
We work at desks.
We can shorten our names
or take new ones. We look swell
in bow ties and bobby sox,
go mad over baseball,
sports cars, and convertibles.

All we have to do, mamma,
is plan to enjoy ourselves,
lighten up about
the old days.

Much has been done
that was promised.
It cost us, sure,
tanti morti.
Fatto! We're still alive, see.
Right here, where we are
is freedom. We got it.
And we're dancin'.

No one wants to board
the last boat back
to the Old Country.

ritual:

ice ponds crack to

robin-song

Sixty Years Ago

I will never forget my surprise
at finding them
in such profusion
and in such an unlikely place
my first spring
in the town.
They swept down the hill
at the edge of a wood
that bordered the creek.
As I came up
the embankment
in the middle of an afternoon,
I looked to where
the trees broke open.
The glory there!
Half an acre of brilliant-yellow crowns
against black earth,
trumpeting the sun.

March ice:

out the window, I see an oak limb

crash to earth

The Pretty Toys

Each night after we had gone to sleep
she sewed cotton nightgowns for our dolls,
while he built two wooden cradles.
Christmas Eve they tucked the dolls in
and placed them near our bed.

With incredible care, they made toys
that filled our friends with envy.
He cut red leather reins for a hobbyhorse.
She embroidered its head, stuffed it with cotton,
stitched on a yellow yarn mane.

How difficult to believe
what came after—her stash of pills,
the car she crashed two blocks from home,
endless visits to hospitals,
the way he clenched and unclenched his jaw.

But I see clearly that afternoon
my sister found her staring
unconscious on the couch—
that morning before school
she'd thrown me against the wall—

senseless from prescription drugs,
body bloated, hair almost gone
under wigs of blonde or brown or red—
those after-dinner shots he gave
before tucking her in.

—continued

Once when I visited near her death,
he and I talked about all the toys,
how sad they'd gotten lost.
I asked how long he could minister,
why he didn't hire help.

"How long?" he repeated,
voice turned steely,
eyes dropping to his cigarette.
"I remember the good times as well as you do."

too steep

this frozen path—

no one behind me

II

Walking on Ice

From the hand-bound book
I tore out several pages
Changing the story line.

Listen, now, the gentle tone
Of your voice, sharp tongue.

Rain

Days she talked so loud
even their senile
Irish Setter winced—

this summer too much rain
cabin too small
wood walls too damp in the heat
and the sheets—not fresh anymore

last year
he'd loved the rain.

July thunder—

at the curb a car alarm's

false warning

Holding On

At first it seems we'll see this all again
until we know how it goes
though we can't quite grasp it now
January too long summer too short
too much rain last year not enough now

we watch each other gather spouses kids degrees
sit in our kitchens and play solitaire
betting on better tomorrows
hugging our knees we try to remember
what it was we missed try to see it new

moved by cool jazz in the afternoon
at the concert in the parking lot
all the way home
we're sure we've got it
everything slips into the rhythm

when we reach the kitchen door
the bass goes mute ivories falter
the ice blue sound melts down and out
we're standing once again
in space that has no sides

"We need

a peaceful movie,"

she shouts.

Fools

The jester is sick
of his own jokes,
but he tumbles, tells
his best stories, tries
to keep the queen content.
In time, no one can tell
a laugh from a lie.

"This isn't funny anymore,"
the queen complains.
More and more jokes seem
to be on her. "What does
the little drudge want?"
she mutters.

She stomps, enraged,
in tears at being banished
from the privilege of pride,
furious to see the fool's
shadow limping along
behind a candlelit curtain.
Pacing, cap in hand,
he hears the even, iron
sound of guards approaching,
feels his cap slipping
from his fingers,
the floor beginning
to tilt away.

Plunging through the drape,
the queen careens into him.
They tumble on well-scrubbed
stone, fingernails sinking
into velvet, wrists tangled
in ribbons—locked in an
endless embrace.

Safety

Silence gets broken
when a heart crashes,

and only if you're
there to hear it.

Let us keep apart then.

moving day—

only the mother longs

for a last look

Flight

The bluebird
lost three
of his finest
feathers between
Puget Sound

and Petaluma.
In his breast
sounded a
weighty gong.

Dusk took his
one good eye
in obedience
to the night.

The Tryout

Seals were barking at a fat spider in the corner
of the basement window. The eight-foot floodwaters
were calm, so the seals could see her slightest move.
Their enthusiasm excited the spider. Stepping into
slippers, she twirled round her web like a Sufi.
Outside the sun sat in a windless sky above miles
of stagnant streams. The only sound, a burst of
applause—and tiny tapping feet.

little girl

wears her mother's shoes—

big as any adult

Taking You Home

Old people repeat themselves
everyone knows that
but it was tormenting anyway
to have you ask every day

to see the farm of your childhood
three miles from the crossroads
where you were living
when I came to look after you

still I drove you every week
over the same ruts
you and your brothers
had walked your horse along

until we saw the house
in the middle of the field
windows broken, wind-scoured wood
front door a hole above the stoop

caved-in roof splitting
the oldness of you Father
on those September days
chills my mind—the earth

did not wait till summer
to return you to itself
how I hated
to take you home

dapple-gray ponies

blue morning glories

share the split-rail fence

The Litchfield Hatchery

Too weary even to think
about staying or leaving,
I began to feel faint, but
glad to see again the town
square, small stone church,
one road in and out.

From a wooden bench I watched
a king-cab pickup gulp gas
at the Shell across the tar road.
How long ago had the hatchery
been replaced by holding tanks?

I stared a long time in the slanting sun
before noticing Sven Hanson—
who'd passed on in '48—waving.

I put down my purse and crossed
the road. "Afternoon, Nora," Sven
said. "Come back to see 'em, yah?"
He rolled up the station's door,
revealing thousands of noisy
chicks in trays.

The smell of warm down filled
the air. It was like walking into
a cloud, some gathering of clouds,
perfect creamy bodies, beaks eager
as when I was a girl.

—continued

I'd taken them into cities and towns
never forgetting these cheeping newborn,
local farmers' pride, long years of waiting
to find again what I had lost
here at circle's end.

tart McIntosh—

inside the barn below me

apple pressing

On the Road

And now summer has gone, and empty flowerpots
yawn at the local folks as they pass. I am the only
stranger here. It's not like I'd remembered: apple
orchards, lots of children, a lake maybe. But it's all
dried up, and cold—I'd forgotten September. Heads
bent against the wind. Still, in the evening Dad's
small half-duplex warm, and local newscasts on his
TV let me believe I could belong here. If not here,
somewhere on the road.

On Wishing Myself a New Life

It comes to me a morning in May
back in Michigan
as the moving van swings onto the Interstate
that fifty years of memories packed
        in cartons on this van

are so much lint—
soft caps, bright mittens you knit
to warm the tiny veins of my fingers
one white winter after another,
before over-prescribed pills savaged you, Mother,
        froze your senses,

delicate bracelet you tooled
to encircle my small-child's wrist,
these last months of your life, Father,
        you cannot stand

the sight of me—
twenty-five-year-old playbill I preserved
to prove we met, my dear, and fell in love
as Pirandello players.
        Here on the seat beside me,

—continued

fresh divorce papers.
As I follow Bekins close
to the Straits of Mackinac,
and approach the 8,000-foot suspension bridge,
I see the wind come rushing,
waving us onto the main span,
        but a blackening sky holds me back—

new to these parts, the Bekins' driver
barrels on, making it halfway
before the wind reaches its arms
under the king-size truck,
lifts it above the center truss,
        and tosses it over the rail—

Eight double wheels spinning wildly in the air—
the Great Lakes close over everything.

Dry leaves crumble
before the wind's
sigh.

Not even pity can
put them together.

All this worrying
won't do.

Lost

Dreaming again of being lost
on streets that meet always
at the same noisy intersection
of downtown buildings
the same bus appears
I get on
the seats are empty
the sun closes down
night quickly opens
and fills fields with dark
the bus rolls
through empty country
withdrawing like an idea
I once had
of a remembered house
with people waiting
behind thin doors
I thought
I could enter

snowdrift,

such bleak mounds . . .

family graves

The lake ice glares,

wild shadows outside my door—

wolf moon!

Walking on Ice

Just below the ice, I'm sure
I hear Lake Superior running.

One of the chilled trout near
the top calls out to me, her

mouth filled with words
that bubble, bump

against April's ceiling.
I lean closer to meet the

eye she turns up, but
cannot tell whether

she warns of hairline cracks
or is trying to remind me

that any hidden rift
can sink a mortal heart.

III

Foot Soldiers

sun kisses the wings

of the hummingbird . . .

singing chimes

Maytime

a silver cage carries Persephone
swinging
across the night sky

tears
soft as kisses
soak the parched earth

only the nightingale
notices
her shining return

our love came

as a surprise

    and still is

Il Divino

We meet on the marble balcony.
Putti fly out of your Florentine-silk scarf,
sneeze on the dust of Michelangelo's *Slaves*.
Scent of fresh roses saturates old air.

Red robes muffle princely footsteps
on the tricolored floor far below us.
Soundless Vespa X9's encircle
columns radiant with chiseled light.

Troops of Jews mill around the *Moses*;
one climbs up on the *Madonna*'s lap.
Laughter is heard in the great hall.
Banners wave: "Il Divino, Il Divino."

Offering a lukewarm prayer,
we kiss our hands and wave back
at a blue angel we can barely see,
pushing through clouds.

in Donnini Forest

a cuckoo calls . . .

our last day

Starfish brighten
the beach.

Wavelets lick
the shore.

In love at noon—
burning sand.

meadowlark—

my day begins

in flute-song

missing signs

of a long summer, rivers drift

into drought

Mouse Tales

Mouse tales told late at night, underneath the cellar stairs. The chattering of their teeth. Upstairs the old man squats on his bedpan. Everyone has a story to tell when the lights are out.

In Search of Kasey

in memory of Janet

Years of nervous defiance numbed your family's
concerns. Your escalating tantrums were a cry for help,
but then, you'd always been high-strung. You wanted
to be brightest teacher, longest-suffering spouse,
matchless mother but could not save your fetal-alcohol
students, boozer husband. The terror you felt when
Kasey died at age nine stayed in your bones.

"She's an angel, waiting for me"—your certainty
frightened clerks and waiters. You filled your house
with angels: ceramic, cotton, straw, tin. You gulped
Coca-Cola, gobbled pills, lost half your stomach—
then, in search of your daughter, you killed the
stranger who was yourself.

Foot Soldiers

Bread's in the oven, chicken's in the pen,
it all seems futile, 'til the rains come again.
It all seems futile, like the falling of the sky,
but I guess we'll make it through, if the river don't dry.

When the women gather 'round, the men start to sing.
It all seems futile, 'til the comin' on of spring.
Grandma wore a blue skirt, mother wore a green,
and I wear a patchwork, like the comin' on of spring.

Cousin Richard's son didn't shoot himself,
and Janet isn't dead, and we'll all march together
in shoes made of lead.

old cherry tree,

few petals to shed—

ducklings fill the pond

School Days

1945

A balmy October blows
through the classroom. Eager faces
turn toward the teacher.

On a bulletin board
paper pumpkins grin at a forty-eight-star flag
standing near the cloakroom door.

The teacher, almost fifty,
wears a wool sweater,
holds a book of rhymes.

And the whole room rings:
"Over in the meadow
in the sand in the sun,
lived an old mother turtle
and her little turtle one."

2005

On the news this wintry afternoon
children are screaming. A wild-eyed boy
throws gravel at the camera.

On the frostbitten lawn
teachers turn students away—a body
lies near the flagpole's base.

—continued

The reporter, almost thirty,
wears an orange blazer,
lifts a roving mike.

Helicopters muffle her announcement:
"Here in this quiet town
a ten-year-old's gun
has killed the first-grade son
of this school's librarian."

On winter nights, dense fog
Covers the moon, hiding a garden
From wandering deer.

Scrambling down the mountain through wailing wind
I'm forced to think of cherry blossoms.

again this year

narcissus in full flower

beside the shrinking pond

The Jump

in memoriam

Under the orange-red bridge
Triton trumpets enshrouded sea,
plays an intricate motif,
    with flat passion
        in melancholy meter,

as though dark were forever,
as though to hear his horn
in this black tunnel
    is a privilege given
        only this night.

Your mother says she listens
every winter's eve
when the Bay is blanketed in fog,
    and the Golden Gate
        is only hazy yellow lights.

For five years, Triton's brought her
close enough to catch the scrape
of your feet off the railing—
    to stare at the tempest slapping
        your teenaged body.

All night she is there with you.
    She's nowhere else
        to go.

crows,

not charmed by meadowlarks,

sound out of sorts

Deepest Dark

We have not called the sea,
but up she comes
showing off for the shore,
too busy tossing waves
to see the storm coming.
      Hellish!
      Hellish! Hellish!
in four hours 400,000 tons of
oil flood her deepest dark,

soundlessly ride her engulfing
folds all the way to daylight.
Wind-driven, bending in pain,
vomiting masses of dead
gulls onto her beaches, she
crashes wave after keening
wave in unholy dread for
clam, walrus, lobster,
starfish, worm, and weed—
passes swollen hands over

otters too small to survive
the suffocating slick. A pup
lifts his blackened body
to the beach, moves his
glazed head from side to side.

—continued

In the hour before nightfall,
we hold on for our lives
to the rocky sea wall,
petroleum lapping our boots.
Oiled snakes circle a rising
surf. A tarred four-ton
white shark rages
fifty yards from shore.

What if we offer up
"a handsome sacrifice"?
What if we pray hard for
all the gods' help?
If we plead
      Innocent!
      Innocent! Innocent!
—will the gods listen?

Judgment Day

Split hairs split hairs
get the details down
build villages of minutia

pursue trifles
bring lanterns to light
the labyrinth of mirrors

census the stars
measure black holes
pin every species to your board

when you've tabulated all
don't waste a minute
climb the steps of the asylum

hold your thimble carefully
not to spill a drop
if the inmates judge it good

your work is done you're free
to lift the edge of darkness
slip beneath its veil

No One Sees

No one is out this late.
No one sees the beach blacken
under the moon,
grunion frantic on the sand.
Even the clams are
frightened. Framework
for a titanic hotel
gleams atop the cliff.

Wind wears itself out
against the giant rib cage,
salt air scrapes steel bones,
uneasy cormorants
throw shadows across
broad beams,
chill mists envelop
the welded shell.

Rainpools on tarpaulins
reflect the clouding moon
like murky mirrors.
In the growing darkness,
no one hears Scylla's
ferocious baying—
pulling us forward
faster and faster.

IV

How Gentleness Came

let bitter wind

show you how to rest . . .

a still summer day

At China Cove
after Mary Oliver

At China Cove
the sea curls
her white fingers
over the soft beach

and easily coaxes
a line of sand
into the blue water.
Close to shore

an otter is floating
like a buoyant toy,
ice plants spreading over cliff tops—
red crowns in the sun.

When I go back home
to the southwest—
to the long-dry sea beds—
to easy comparisons I might make

between ocean and arroyo,
I must shut my office door—
I must pick up my pen—
I must step back

—continued

onto the lost beach,
on which I am moving now
like a shorebird,
a coyote,

so content,
I am almost the ice plant—
almost the bird sweeping over the sand
from its slice of sky.

plunging neckline—

the poet reads from

Songs of Innocence

A Visit from God

I saw You come at me in a taffeta skirt
and orange sneakers,
cymbals and drums banging,
Your guffaw
bouncing off canyon walls
as You pitched the sun
round the earth.

"That's some getup,
special occasion?" I asked.
"You're it," God bellowed,
jamming a silver bell
into my pocket.

"So you should ring Me sometime,
no need to look in the Book.
You make Me happy, you know.
You can see how I'm dressed up,
but you're off the track—
you gotta make more noise
about Me."

"Well," I say, "I'm not
much of a shouter."
"Listen," God says, "maybe
it's time. Here, take a drum,
make yourself of some use."

—continued

So, there we were,
strutting along the seashore,
me beating this Japanese drum,
and God making fat footprints
in the sand.

Blown in wide circles
By the breezes
Of springtime—
Loose down of cottonwood.

Seeds having scattered, orioles
Hang their nests from upper branches.

raindrops on windows—

how precious these rare jewels

builders thirst after

Status

This noon a thrasher
struts along
the adobe wall

noisily in his bravest
showing of pride and all
it means to him

to be the best,
the busiest builder
in this gated subdivision.

real estate boom

local market crescendos—

after we sell

The Embrace

A chill April morning
nudges me through the greenbelt
onto a still-frozen footpath
next to the rancher's fence,
and I think the usual
about fortuity and freedom:
how it is good to stand on the land,
how good to breathe this thin air.

The delicate tint of sky—
Botticelli's master—
orders me to stare up,
and I wonder how it might feel
to be one of the artist's Nativity angels
circling a painted sky with careless feet,
swirling with dancing sleeves,
curls caught in bright breezes,
all those hosannas hurrying high and higher

into pure, pale blue—
how it might feel
to wing down wildly
to embrace a jubilant mortal—
I cast first shadows,
hear the meadowlark sing—
feel sweet fingers touch
my shivering shoulders.

evening stroll

gold chamisas stun at sunset—

our happy chatter

burning desert gusts

blowing away

last night's sleep

Endgame

Birds are vanishing
we know listen
hear them winging

see them gather
sleepless
in forgotten trees

while we stand
in withered rows
waiting for song

deep autumn . . .

cold even at noon

my wrinkled skin

coyotes yelp

clouds hug the mountaintops—

quilts up to chins

on and on the clouds . . .

everywhere I look

snow keeps falling

A Black Heaven

The sky is lumpy this morning.
Grey-blue and black, the clouds
cover the sun, fatten, and cling
to the mountains. Fearsome
in its thunder and lightning
the sky pretends its pacific blue
is gone for good. Look how easily
we make its story our own,
told the only way to live now
is under a black heaven, drenched
in the terror of lies or clinging
full of pride
to our blood-soaked precipice.

from my sickbed

I hear crows squawk in praise

of prickly pears

bomb's whistle—

the sound of

keening

wounded desert lark:

a widow hovers over

her dying children

No End in Sight

Rabbits wear name tags to the bottom of the hill. When they reach the clover, one refuses to keep his tag on. In this time of Burrow Patrols, news of the traitor multiplies. It is nothing he doesn't understand. He's heard of this in another time of terror. He expects to be dragged off. Still, he is surprised and shaken to see so many scuffling, groveling rabbits at the secret trial dressed as sheep.

"Look at them—so white, they must blacken their names to be true to our homeland," croaks an aging suspect, sheared, hanging by his bruised hind feet.

Iraq . . .

so many deaths

intestate

Light

The moon has come full up;
stars cannot compete. When

dark nights overtake us, we'll
flick our flashlights on,

sure of where we are
in that small circle of light.

steady slant of rain

bends every bush—

arroyo water up to my ankles

holy water:

month of the Sangré's Blue Lake

snowmelt

how like

a cherry tree in blossom

the young girl's haiku

Contentment

Light fills this small bowl,
       will the rim dare to defy it?
A curve can be any embrace,
       the difference made by turning.

how simple . . .

coming up out of the arroyo

six deer

The Way Gentleness Came

When the summer rain stops,
I touch a drenched peony
like the skin
of my grandmother's cheek
where tears crept into creases,
her voice faint,
a lullaby on the breeze,

falling weightless, the way
gentleness came over me
like easy breathing
our last afternoon
on the step
of the wood porch
where the black pump stood.

I watch her walk up
from the garden
holding a bucket of beans
in the crook of her arm
against the bulging bodice
of a faded homemade dress,
half-shut eyes

—continued

squint against the sun
to see me there.
Soft, wrinkled flesh
of her round face
lifts at the mouth
as she speaks my name

like a mourning dove's call
when first light shines
through silver rain.
Fixing her smile on mine,
she quickens her step,
tears at the edges of eyes
seeping into my own.

startled—

at the stoplight

a whoosh of finches

after twenty years

still your bighearted way

of loving me

First Blossoms

Now that spring has come
to lead me home again,
I hold it to its promise
to make something brighter
of my days: to turn on birdsong,
turn up the sun, sprinkle
lupine in the field. And then,
when the swelling stream
has broken through the ice,
to hurry my heart to surface,
fill my outstretched hands
with yellow swallowtails,
dance me to the garden
where the apple tree blooms,
shake baskets of first blossoms
on my already-white hair.

for just a moment

I put my ear to the ground—

oh, ancient river!

And with Fondness...

"American Beauty" is for Gisela Bailin

"Epidemic: 1949" is for Gayle Snyder

"In Search of Kasey" is for Michael Scofield

"The Jump" is for Nancy Sears

"The Way Gentleness Came" is for Jennifer Galanis and
Brendan Ward

Printed in the United States
218930BV00001B/23/P

9 780865 346550